Contents

A colourful country

White snow covers the peaks of the Himalayas in the north of India. The sandy yellow dunes of the Thar Desert cover the northwest. Goa's blue-water beaches attract visitors to the west coast. India is a colourful country tucked into the southern part of the continent of Asia. It is bordered by Pakistan and China in the north, and Nepal, Bhutan, Myanmar (Burma), and Bangladesh to the east. The rest of the country juts out into the Indian Ocean.

Mehrangarh Fort overlooks the Jaswant Thada mausoleum and the city of Jodhpur in the state of Rajasthan.

Throughout its history, India has attracted outsiders. India was known for its spices, silks, and other goods. Many other countries wanted to trade with or control India. In the 1500s, the Mughals conquered most of India and ruled it for more than 300 years. The Portuguese controlled parts of the west. British took control of most of India until 1947, when it finally became its own independent country.

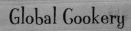
Global Cookery

Recipes
From

India

Dana Meachen Rau

raintree
a Capstone company — publishers for children

Raintree is an imprint of Capstone Global Library Limited, a company incorporated in England and Wales having its registered office at 7 Pilgrim Street, London, EC4V 6LB – Registered company number: 6695582

www.raintreepublishers.co.uk
myorders@raintreepublishers.co.uk

Text © Capstone Global Library Limited 2014
First published in hardback in 2014
Paperback edition first published in 2015
The moral rights of the proprietor have been asserted.

Edited by Abby Colich, Laura Knowles, and John-Paul Wilkins
Designed by Cynthia Akiyoshi
Picture research by Tracy Cummins
Production by Vicki Fitzgerald
Originated by Capstone Global Library
Printed and bound in China

ISBN 978 1 406 27380 9 (hardback)
17 16 15 14 13
10 9 8 7 6 5 4 3 2 1

ISBN 978 1 406 27385 4 (paperback)
18 17 16 15 14
10 9 8 7 6 5 4 3 2 1

A full catalogue record for this book is available from the British Library.

Acknowledgments
We would like to thank the following for permission to reproduce photographs: Capstone Publishers pp. 1, 9–11, 16–43 (Karon Dubke); © Crown p.12 (copyright material is reproduced with the permission of HMSO and Queen's Printer for Scotland, food.gov.uk); Getty Images pp. 13 (Tetra Images), 15 (Granefelt, Lena); Shutterstock pp. 4 (Boris Stroujko), 5 (Malgorzata Kistryn), 6 (AJP), 14 (Gayvoronskaya_Yana); Superstock p. 7 (PictureIndia).

Design elements reproduced with permission of Shutterstock (Andrey Savin, Brooke Becker, Dmitrij Skorobogatov, Fedorov Oleksiy, foodonwhite, fotostoker, Igor Plotnikov, Jayakumar Llaszlo, Luis Santos, Maks Narodenko, marchello74, Mazzzur, nito, photastic, Picsfive, Richard Peterson, saiko3p, Sandra Cunningham).

Cover photograph of a saag paneer reproduced with permission of Capstone Publishers (Karon Dubke).

We would like to thank Sarah Schenker and Marla Conn for their invaluable help in the preparation of this book.

The author would like to thank Aditya and Eileen for their invaluable advice.

An Indian family brings food home from a market in Mumbai. Many Indians have to survive on very basic ingredients.

Today, Indians share many cultural and historical traditions. But they are a varied people as well. While most Indians speak the language Hindi, there are nearly 400 other languages. Most Indians practise the religion of Hinduism, but there are many other religions, too.

India is packed with people farming in villages or working in the cities. In fact, India has the second-largest population of any country in the world. A crowded city is a colourful and flavourful display, especially in the markets selling spices.

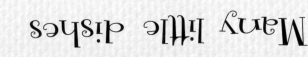

Many little dishes

The combination of spices adds distinct flavours to Indian foods. Spices such as cumin, cardamom, and cinnamon blend into aromas that are uniquely Indian. But not all foods in this large country are the same. In the north, food can be rich with lots of onion and garlic. Southern foods are often spicier since chilli peppers grow in the south. Coastal areas use seafood and coconut in their dishes.

The Mughals brought meat dishes to the north, but many Indians are vegetarians. They do not eat meat for religious or cultural reasons. Other food traditions have come from the many settlers and invaders of India's past.

Fresh seafood is sold daily at this huge street market in the state of Kerala.

An Indian meal includes many dishes. Instead of being served in separate courses, these dishes are served all at once. This is called a *thali* meal. Choices may include a meat or vegetable dish with yogurt. Lentils are cooked into a smooth paste. Pickles, salads, and jam-like chutneys accompany the meal. Bread is eaten along with meals in the north, and rice is more common in the south.

There is a wide variety of flavours in Indian food. This family is eating bread with a tasty selection of condiments.

These meals are often served "family-style". Food is placed in the centre of a table or on a mat on the floor. People sit around it and take what they want. Indians scoop up and mix food with the fingertips of the right hand or with a piece of bread.

Indian ingredients

Here are some ingredients found in Indian households and in the recipes in this book. If you can't find a certain ingredient, look for similar replacements.

Rice is a staple food of the south. Indians prefer long grain and basmati, which has a nutty taste and floral scent.

Flours, such as chapati flour, are used to make traditional Indian breads. You can use white and wheat flour, too.

Spices are probably the most important part of Indian cooking. Some of the most common include peppercorns, cardamom, cayenne (ground dry red chillies), cinnamon, cloves, coriander, cumin, fennel, fenugreek, mustard seeds, saffron, and turmeric.

Herbs also provide unique flavours to curries and other dishes. These include bay leaves, coriander leaves (cilantro), curry leaves, and mint.

Garam masala is a roasted spice mix that most Indians make fresh. It usually contains cumin, coriander, cinnamon, cardamom, and cloves.

Ginger, garlic, and green peppers add an extra spicy bite to many dishes.

Fruits play a part in main dishes, condiments, and desserts in India. Commonly used fruits include mangoes, watermelon, coconuts, limes, and lemons.

Vegetables are important because so many Indians are vegetarians. Popular vegetables include cauliflower, cucumber, aubergine, okra, peas, potatoes, and spinach.

Nuts, such as cashews, pistachios, and almonds, and dried fruit, such as raisins and apricots, are eaten as desserts or used to garnish dishes.

Pulses are legumes, such as lentils, dried beans, or split peas, that provide protein.

Yogurt is a part of most meals and provides a cool taste alongside a spicy dish.

Paneer is a homemade cheese used in main dishes and desserts. It has a dense, crumbly texture that combines well with the strong flavours in Indian cooking. You can find a recipe for paneer on page 22.

Meat, poultry, and fish are not a part of every Indian's diet. Goat is the most common meat eaten. Chicken and lamb are also popular. Fish and shellfish are well liked on the coasts.

Ghee is a fat used widely in Indian cooking. It is a type of clarified butter, made by simmering butter and removing the residue that rises to the top. You can use vegetable oil instead.

The Indian diet is filled with healthy foods and exotic spices.

How to use this book

Each chapter of this book will introduce you to aspects of Indian cooking. But you don't have to read the book from beginning to end. Flip through, find what interests you, and give it a try. You may discover a recipe that becomes your new favourite meal!

Tandoori chicken

A tandoor is a traditional clay oven, fuelled with wood or coal. It is common in Punjab in northern India. Indians use the tandoor to make flatbreads and meats. But you can use your oven for this recipe. Marinating the chicken in yogurt is not only important for flavour. It helps tenderize, or soften, the chicken, too.

Ingredients

4 skinless, boneless chicken thighs (about 700 g)
180 ml plain non-fat yogurt
1 tablespoon minced root ginger
6 cloves garlic, minced
1 tablespoon lemon juice
½ teaspoon salt
Non-stick cooking spray
Red onion, sliced
Lemon, sliced

Spices

¼ teaspoon cayenne
2 teaspoons paprika
1 teaspoon cumin
1 teaspoon coriander
½ teaspoon cardamom

Tools

Measuring jug and spoons
Blender or food processor
Knife
Bowl
Cling film
Baking dish

If you already do a lot of cooking, you may know your way around the kitchen. But if you've never grated cucumber, pureed a mango, or sautéed onions, don't worry. Have a look at the glossary on page 44.

Each recipe is set up the same way: Ingredients lists all the ingredients you'll be adding. Tools tells you the various kitchen utensils you will need. Collect the ingredients and tools before you start working so that you have everything nearby when you need it.

Then just follow the Steps. Make sure you read them carefully. Numbers on the photos indicate which step they refer to. Don't worry if your creation isn't perfect when you reach the end. Cooking takes practice and experimentation. Be patient and enjoy the process.

If you have to follow a specific diet, or have food allergies, look for the labels on each recipe. These will tell you if a dish is vegan, vegetarian, dairy-free, gluten-free, or if it contains nuts or coconut. However, you should always check food packaging before use to be sure.

Steps

1. In a blender or food processor, blend the yogurt, ginger, garlic, lemon juice, salt and spices into a smooth sauce.

2. Cut diagonal slits in the chicken pieces and place in a bowl. Pour the sauce over the chicken, mixing it well with your hands. Make sure the pieces are covered and the sauce gets into the slits.

3. Cover the bowl with cling film and place in the refrigerator for 1 to 24 hours. Stir it occasionally to make sure all the pieces are fully coated in the marinade.

4. Spray a baking dish with non-stick cooking spray. Place the chicken in a single layer in the dish.

5. Bake at 200°C for about 30 minutes, turning once during cooking, until the chicken is cooked through.

6. Serve with slices of onion and lemon.

Makes 4 servings
Time: 10 minutes prep, up to
    24 hours marinating,
    30 minutes baking

2a

2b

Quick tip

Indians often buy spices whole, and then grind them into a powder themselves. This brings out the most flavour. But you can buy most spices already ground, too.

VARIATION

You can also cook this chicken on an outdoor grill to give it a barbeque flavour. Cook the pieces at medium heat for about 5 to 7 minutes per side, or until cooked through.

19

N contains nuts

D airy free

G luten free

V egetarian

V egan

C contains oconut

Look at Quick tips for cooking and kitchen advice, and Variations for swapping ingredients for others if you would like.

Whenever you are in the kitchen, ask an adult to help or be nearby. You shouldn't use any knife or appliance without an adult's permission and assistance. You can find more ways to be safe while you cook on page 14.

A healthy kitchen

It's fun to head out on a food adventure by trying new tastes from countries beyond your own. But you should also keep your health in mind. The following are the basic food groups. Indians include all of these groups in a meal, or over the course of a day, to get the proper balance of nutrients to grow and be healthy.

Fruits and vegetables

Indians may enjoy a bite of watermelon to cool off on a hot day, or mix mango into spicy and sweet dishes. Vegetables are also a very important part of the Indian diet. They are cooked into curry sauces or sautéed in spices. Both fruits and vegetables can help reduce the risk of getting certain diseases. They contain nutrients your body needs and fibre to keep your digestive system running smoothly.

Grains

These are foods made from wheat, rice, corn, oats, or other grains. Whole grains that use the entire grain kernel are the healthiest. Refined grains, such as white flour and white rice, do not have as many vitamins and minerals. Rice and bread are in this group.

The eatwell plate

Use the eatwell plate to help you get the balance right. It shows how much of what you eat should come from each food group.

food.gov.uk

Fruit and vegetables

Flakes

Bread, rice, potatoes, pasta and other starchy foods

Meat, fish, eggs, beans and other non-dairy sources of protein

Foods and drinks high in fat and/or sugar

Milk and dairy foods

The eatwell plate shows us the importance of eating a combination of all the food groups in our diets.

Try Indian dishes to discover lots of tasty new flavours!

Protein

Protein foods include meats, poultry, and seafood. They also include pulses (such as lentils) and nuts.

Dairy

Milk and any products made from milk fall into this category. Dairy foods contain a lot of bone-building calcium. The homemade cheese paneer is part of this group. Yogurt is a popular source of calcium for Indians.

Fats and sugar

Some oils, especially the ones from plants, like vegetable oil, do provide some important nutrients. Nuts are high in oils, too. But solid fats, such as butter and meat fat, are not as good for you. So use them sparingly. Your body needs sugar, but not too much. Try not to fill up on too many Indian sweets!

A safe kitchen

It's fun to whip up a tasty new creation in the kitchen, but safety should be your number one concern. Here are some tips to keep in mind:

- Make sure an adult is nearby for permission, help, advice, and assistance.
- Wash your hands before you work.
- Wear the right clothing, including sturdy shoes and an apron.
- Foods can grow harmful bacteria. Make sure you keep foods in the refrigerator or freezer until they are ready to use. Check expiration dates. If something smells or looks funny, it may be spoiled.

Remember to wash knives and chopping boards after you use them with raw meat.

Watch your fingers and don't rush when you use a knife.

- Raw meat, poultry, seafood, and eggs can carry germs. Always wash your hands immediately after touching them. Wash any knife or chopping board after you use them with these foods. Make sure these foods are cooked all the way through before you eat them. Clean worktops and kitchen tools with warm, soapy water when you have finished working.

- On the hob, make sure pan handles point in, so the pans don't get knocked over. Never leave pans unattended. Do not let anything flammable, such as loose sleeves or tea towels, near burners on the hob.

- Always use oven gloves when removing something from the oven or microwave. Avoid steam when you lift a top off a pan on the hob or in the oven.

- Knives are sharp. Always point the blade away from you. Take your time and pay attention to what you are cutting. Don't use a knife without the help of an adult.

Masala meals

Masala means "spice" in the Indian language Hindi. Indian meals often are either dry masalas (seasoned with dry spices) or wet masalas (started from a mixture of wet ingredients, such as tomatoes or onion, and spices). Either way, spice is central to the following popular meat meals of India.

Coconut prawn curry

Coconut trees grow well in India's southern tropical climate, so many dishes from this region include coconut milk. Curries are a popular way to serve seafood, as well as many other meats and vegetables. *Curry* means "sauce", and can be mild or spicy.

Ingredients

700 g uncooked large prawns, shelled, deveined, and washed

1 tablespoon vegetable oil

1 medium onion, chopped

1 tablespoon minced root ginger

6 cloves garlic, minced

2 tablespoons chopped green chillies (or to taste)

1 teaspoon salt

1 (400-ml) can coconut milk

Spices

1½ teaspoons coriander

1½ teaspoons cumin

Tools

Kitchen scales

Measuring spoons

Frying pan

Steps

1. Heat the oil in a frying pan on medium-high. Add the onion and cook for about 8 to 10 minutes.

2. Add the ginger, chillies, and garlic, and sauté for about a minute more. Then add the salt and spices and stir them to combine.

3. Pour in the coconut milk. Turn up the heat and bring the sauce to the boil. Then reduce to medium, and cook, uncovered, for about 5 to 8 minutes, stirring frequently. The sauce will thicken.

4. Add the prawns. Cook for about 3 to 5 minutes until the prawns turn pink and are cooked through. Serve with rice (see rice tips on page 30).

Quick tip

To make mincing garlic and ginger easier, you can use a grater with small holes instead of a knife. The grater will mince the ginger and garlic for you. But be careful of your fingers when you get near the end.

You can hold onto the hard tails when you are eating prawns. Just eat the flesh and set the tails aside.

Makes 4 servings
Time: About 30 minutes

Dairy free   Gluten free   contains Coconut

17

Tandoori chicken

A tandoor is a traditional clay oven, fuelled with wood or coal. It is common in Punjab in northern India. Indians use the tandoor to make flatbreads and meats. But you can use your oven for this recipe. Marinating the chicken in yogurt is not only important for flavour. It helps tenderize, or soften, the chicken, too.

Ingredients

4 skinless, boneless chicken thighs (about 700 g)
180 ml plain fat free yogurt
1 tablespoon minced root ginger
6 cloves garlic, minced
1 tablespoon lemon juice
½ teaspoon salt
Non-stick cooking spray
Red onion, sliced
Lemon, sliced

Spices

¼ teaspoon cayenne
2 teaspoons paprika
1 teaspoon cumin
1 teaspoon coriander
½ teaspoon cardamom

Tools

Measuring jug and spoons	Bowl
Blender or food processor	Cling film
Knife	Baking dish

Steps

1. In a blender or food processor, blend the yogurt, ginger, garlic, lemon juice, salt and spices into a smooth sauce.

2. Cut diagonal slits in the chicken pieces and place in a bowl. Pour the sauce over the chicken, mixing it well with your hands. Make sure the pieces are covered and the sauce gets into the slits.

3. Cover the bowl with cling film and place in the refrigerator for 1 to 24 hours. Stir it occasionally to make sure all the pieces are fully coated in the marinade.

4. Spray a baking dish with non-stick cooking spray. Place the chicken in a single layer in the dish.

5. Bake at 200°C for about 30 minutes, turning once during cooking, until the chicken is cooked through.

6. Serve with slices of onion and lemon.

2 a

2 b

Makes 4 servings
Time: 10 minutes prep, up to 24 hours marinating, 30 minutes baking

Gluten free

Quick tip

Indians often buy spices whole, and then grind them into a powder themselves. This brings out the most flavour. But you can buy most spices already ground, too.

VARIATION

You can also cook this chicken on an outdoor grill to give it a barbeque flavour. Cook the pieces at medium heat for about 5 to 7 minutes per side, or until cooked through.

Lamb vindaloo

Vindaloo is a speciality of the state of Goa, where the Portuguese colonists settled. *Vindaloo* means "vinegar" and "garlic" in Portuguese. Traditionally, this extremely hot and spicy dish is made from pork. But it is also popular cooked with lamb.

Ingredients

700 g lamb, cut into 2.5-cm pieces
1 tablespoon vegetable oil
1 medium onion, chopped
1 tablespoon minced root ginger
12 cloves garlic, minced
4 tablespoons white vinegar
1 tablespoon tomato paste
½ teaspoon sugar
Water

Spices

2 teaspoons cayenne
2 teaspoons mustard powder
2 teaspoons cumin
2 teaspoons coriander
½ teaspoon ground cinnamon
½ teaspoon ground cloves
½ teaspoon black pepper

Tools

Kitchen scales
Measuring spoons
Frying pan with lid
Blender or food processor

Steps

1. Heat the oil in a frying pan on medium-high. Add the lamb and brown on all sides, turning frequently, for about 5 to 7 minutes. Work in batches if you need to so that the lamb does not crowd the pan. Remove the lamb and set aside.

2. There should still be some oil in the pan. If not, add a little more. Add the onion and sauté on medium for about 10 minutes, until browned and softened.

3. Meanwhile, in a blender or food processor, combine the garlic, ginger, vinegar, tomato paste, sugar, and spices.

4. Add the blended spice mixture to the pan with the onions and cook for about 3 minutes more.

5. Add the lamb back into the pan and mix well. Pour in 120 to 240 ml of water to create a sauce.

6. Bring to the boil, then turn the heat down and simmer covered for about 1½ hours, until the lamb is cooked through.

7. Serve with boiled potatoes or rice (see rice tips on page 30).

Makes 4 servings
Time: 30 minutes prep,
1½ hours to cook

Quick tip

Vindaloo is known for its spiciness. This recipe uses 2 teaspoons of cayenne powder, which makes it very hot. You can adjust the heat as you wish by adding more or less cayenne powder. It's up to you!

Gluten free   **D**airy free

21

Vegetarian dishes

Cows are sacred in Hinduism, the most popular religion in India. This means that Indians do not eat beef. Indian Muslims do not eat pork. Those who practise Jainism, another Indian religion, are forbidden to kill any living creature. Many Indians are vegetarians for cultural or religious reasons. Even those who aren't vegetarians often eat vegetarian dishes.

Paneer

Paneer is homemade Indian cheese. Paneer is very easy to make by separating boiled milk into two parts – curds and whey. When the curds are drained and pressed together, they form a cheese Indians use for main meals and desserts.

Ingredients

1 litre whole milk
1½ tablespoons lemon juice

Tools

Stockpot
Measuring jug and spoons
Wooden spoon
Colander
Thin, clean tea towel or cheesecloth
Stack of plates
Cling film

Steps

1. Bring the milk to the boil over medium heat. Watch it carefully so it doesn't boil over. It will take about 10 minutes.

2. Reduce the heat, and pour in the lemon juice. Stir gently. Almost immediately, the white curds will start to separate from the watery whey. If the whey still looks milky, add a little more lemon juice. The milk should fully separate in about a minute.

3. Place a colander in the sink and line it with a clean towel. Pour the curds and whey into the colander and let the water drain out so only the curds remain.

4. Rinse the curds with cold water. This washes off the lemon flavour and cools the curds so you can handle them.

5. Lift all four corners of the towel out of the colander. Twist the towel closed. Squeeze out as much water from the curds as you can.

6. With the ball of curds still tightly packed inside the towel, flatten and put on a plate. Place a stack of plates on top to squeeze out even more water. Let it sit for about 30 minutes.

7. Unwrap the cheese from the towel. Then wrap the cheese in cling film. Store in the refrigerator until ready to eat. Paneer can be fried in spices and served with chutney, added to curries, or cooked with spinach (see recipe on page 24).

Makes about 150 grams of cheese
Time: About 20 minutes to make,
30 minutes to press

 luten free

 egetarian

23

Saag paneer

Paneer can be fried up and cooked with leafy vegetables to create a satisfying vegetarian dish called saag paneer. This dish is popular in Punjab.

Ingredients

- 1 tablespoon vegetable oil
- About 150 g paneer (see recipe page 22), cut into 2.5-cm cubes
- 1 small onion, chopped
- 1 tablespoon minced root ginger
- 6 cloves garlic, minced
- 1 tablespoon chopped green chillies
- 1 (450-g) packet spinach
- Water
- ½ teaspoon salt
- 120 ml plain fat free yogurt

Spices

- 1 teaspoon cumin
- 1 teaspoon coriander
- ¼ teaspoon cinnamon
- ⅛ teaspoon cloves
- ⅛ teaspoon cayenne

Tools

- Kitchen scales
- Measuring jug and spoons
- Frying pan
- Spatula

Steps

1. Heat the oil in a frying pan on medium-high heat. Add the cubes of paneer. Sauté for about 3 to 5 minutes until browned on all sides. Remove from the pan and set aside.

2. In the same pan, add the onion, ginger, garlic, and chillies. Cook for about 2 minutes to soften. Add the spices and cook another minute.

3. Add the spinach, 60 to 120 ml of water, and salt. Sauté with the other ingredients for about 2 to 3 minutes.

4. Turn the heat down to low. Stir in the yogurt and the fried paneer cubes. Heat another few minutes until the yogurt is warmed through. Serve it with rice or scoop it up with bread.

Quick tips

Preparing ingredients ahead of time makes cooking easier. Measure out all your spices into a bowl before you start cooking. Then when it's time to add them, you don't have to measure out each one and risk something burning in the pan.

To sauté in a pan, use a spoon to move the ingredients around, letting them rest only occasionally, so they cook evenly and do not stick to the bottom.

Makes 4 servings
Time: About 30 minutes

 Gluten free   Vegetarian

Red lentil dal

Dal is any dish made with Indian pulses (such as lentils, beans, and peas) that have been softened by boiling and seasoned with spices. It is one of the most common foods in India. Lentils come in many varieties, such as yellow, green, orange, and black. This dal is made with red lentils. It is an accompaniment to many Indian meals.

Ingredients	Spices	Tools
200 g dried red lentils, sorted and rinsed	½ teaspoon turmeric	Kitchen scales
½ teaspoon salt	1 teaspoon cumin	Measuring jug and spoons
500 ml water	1 teaspoon coriander	Stockpot
2 tablespoons vegetable oil	¼ teaspoon cayenne	Whisk
6 cloves garlic, minced		Small frying pan

Steps

1. Combine the lentils, water, turmeric, and salt in a stockpot. Bring to the boil, and then turn the heat down to low. Cover and simmer the lentils for about 30 to 40 minutes until softened.

2. Whisk lentils in the pot to break them up until smooth.

3. In a small frying pan, heat the oil. Add the garlic, cumin, coriander, and cayenne. Cook for about 2 minutes.

4. Add this flavoured oil to the lentils. Stir well.

5. Scoop up with chapati (see recipe on page 32), or serve as an accompaniment to a rice or any Indian meal.

Quick tip

When you buy dry lentils, they may need to be cleaned first. Rinse the lentils with cold water in a sieve to fully clean them before cooking.

Makes 4 servings
Time: About 50 minutes

 Gluten free

 Dairy free

Vegetarian

 Vegan

Potato and pea samosas

Samosas are a very popular street food in India. People who are in the mood for an afternoon snack might buy this portable treat from a vendor. Samosas are usually deep-fried. Here, they are baked.

Ingredients

2 large white potatoes
2 tablespoons vegetable oil
1 small onion, chopped
1 teaspoon minced root ginger
2 teaspoons chopped green
    chillies
150 g thawed frozen peas
1 packet croissant dough
½ teaspoon salt

Spices

2 teaspoons cumin
1 tablespoon coriander
⅛ teaspoon cinnamon
⅛ teaspoon black pepper

Tools

Kitchen scales	Stockpot
Measuring spoons	Colander
Vegetable peeler	Frying pan
Knife and chopping	Spoon
board	Baking tray

Steps

1. Peel the potatoes and cut them into quarters. Place in a stockpot and cover with water. On high heat, bring them to the boil. Turn down the heat and simmer, covered, for 15 minutes or until potatoes are soft. Drain the potatoes and cut into small cubes.

2. Heat the oil in a pan on medium-high. Add the onion, ginger, chillies, salt, and spices. Cook for about 3 to 5 minutes.

3. Add the potatoes and peas. Cook for another 5 minutes. Set aside.

4. Preheat oven to 190°C.

5. Unroll the croissant dough. Fold the corner of each triangle over and wrap it around the other side to create a funnel shape. Spoon in the filling. Fold over the top flap of dough to seal. Repeat with the rest of the dough.

6. Place the samosas on a baking tray. Bake for about 8 to 10 minutes until lightly browned.

 egetarian

Makes 16 samosas (serves 8)
Time: 40 minutes prep,
10 minutes to bake

Thali tradition

The tradition of serving all the courses at the same time is called a *thali* meal. Thali is actually the name of a large-rimmed plate that contains small bowls with servings of each dish, rice or bread, and various salads, pickles, or chutneys. The courses are eaten together so that the meal is a variety of colours, tastes, smells, and textures. The recipes in this chapter are foods you would find on a thali plate.

Basmati rice

Rice accompanies most meals in southern India. It may be served plain, mixed with a curry, or fried up with spices, onions, or other vegetables into a pilaf. Rice is also an important ingredient in popular breakfast foods, such as *dosas* (crisp, thin pancakes made of ground lentils and rice) and *idlis* (fluffy, steamed rice cakes). Basmati rice grows in the foothills of the Himalayas.

Cooking tips

Rinsing the rice before cooking helps to remove extra starch and keep the grains from sticking together. Soaking helps lessen cooking time and softens the grains. Remember to use a stockpot or saucepan large enough to hold the rice when it expands.

These instructions serve as guidelines only. You should check your packet of rice for cooking directions.

1. To clean the rice, pour it out onto a plate. Pick through it to remove the hulls of the grains or small stones.

2. To rinse the rice, put the rice in a bowl, fill it with cold water, and swish it with your hands. Pour out the milky water (keeping the grains in the bowl with your hand). Repeat 3 or 4 times until the water runs clear.

3. Soak the rice in a bowl of cold water for about 30 minutes. Drain.

4. Put the rice in a stockpot or saucepan. Add about 1½ parts water to 1 part rice.

5. Cover the stockpot with a tight-fitting lid and bring it to the boil. Reduce the heat and simmer for about 10 to 15 minutes, until all the liquid is absorbed.

6. Take off the heat and let it sit for a few minutes. Then fluff it with a fork before serving.

VARIATION

To add flavour to the rice, make a pilaf. Heat about 1 tablespoon of oil in a saucepan and add onion, green chillies, and spices of your choice. Cook for a few minutes. Then add the uncooked dry rice and mix to coat. Add chicken stock instead of water, bring to the boil, then simmer for about 15 to 20 minutes until all the liquid is absorbed.

Chapati

Wheat grows in northern parts of India. So bread, not rice, is served with meals in northern homes. Chapati is a round wheat bread. It is traditionally cooked on a cast iron plate called a tava. But you can make it in a frying pan on the hob.

Ingredients	Tools	
75 g white flour, plus more for dusting	Kitchen scales	Frying pan
75 g wholemeal flour	Measuring jug and spoons	Tongs
60–120 ml water	Large and small bowls	Microwave-safe bowl
3 tablespoons butter	Tea towel	Plate
	Rolling pin	Pastry brush
		Kitchen foil

Steps

1. Using your fingers, combine the flours together in a large bowl. Pour in the water a little at a time and mix it into the flour with your hands until it forms a ball of dough.

2. Lightly dust your work surface with flour so the dough doesn't stick. Knead the dough for about 5 minutes. Put the dough back in the bowl, cover the bowl with a tea towel, and let it rest for about 30 minutes.

3. Place a large frying pan on the hob and heat on medium-high for about 5 minutes, so it gets very hot.

4. Melt the butter in a microwave-safe bowl for about 30 seconds. Set aside.

5. Knead the dough for a bit longer, and then roll it into a rope shape. Cut or break it into 8 equal pieces. Roll each piece into a ball. Then flatten each ball into a disc in your palm.

6. Dust the work surface and rolling pin with flour. Roll the dough into a circle shape about 15 centimetres across.

7. Place the dough in the pan. Cook on one side for 1 minute. The bread will start to puff up. Grab the edge with the tongs, and flip it over. Cook for 1 minute on the other side.

8. Remove the bread from the pan and place on a plate. Brush with the melted butter. Cover with kitchen foil to keep warm while you cook the rest of the chapati.

Makes 8 chapati
Time: About 1 hour 15 minutes

Vegetarian

VARIATION
If you brush the chapati with vegetable oil instead of butter, this recipe can be vegan.

Cucumber raita

Since a lot of Indian food can be spicy, you may need a refreshing dish to calm your taste buds. Raitas are made of yogurt mixed with raw vegetables, cooked vegetables, or fruit and nuts. This cucumber raita helps balance a spicy meal.

Ingredients

1 large cucumber, peeled and grated

240 ml plain fat free yogurt

1 tablespoon chopped green chillies

½ teaspoon cumin

Salt and pepper to taste

Tools

Measuring jug and spoons

Vegetable peeler

Grater

Kitchen roll

Bowl

Whisk

Spoon

Steps

1. Peel and grate the cucumber. Wrap the cucumber in kitchen roll and squeeze out some of the water. Set the cucumber aside.

2. In a bowl, whisk the yogurt until smooth.

3. Add the cucumber, chillies, cumin, and salt and pepper. Mix well.

4. Serve in a bowl as a dipping sauce, or alongside a main meal.

VARIATION

You can also add a diced fresh tomato, or make it spicy by sprinkling in some cayenne.

Makes 6 servings
Time: 10 minutes

Gluten free   **V**egetarian

35

Mango chutney

Chutney is similar to jam. Sometimes it is sweet and fruity. But many types of chutney are also savoury. Indian chutneys can be made of fruit or vegetables. They can taste sweet or sour, or both. Try this sweet and sour chutney made from mangoes and spices. Eat small pieces of it along with your meal.

Ingredients

1 large green (unripe) mango
225 g white sugar
4 tablespoons white vinegar
4 cloves garlic, minced
1 tablespoon minced
    root ginger
¼ teaspoon cayenne (add
    more for extra spice)

Tools

Kitchen scales
Measuring jug
    and spoons
Vegetable peeler
Grater
Saucepan
Spoon

Steps

1. Peel and grate the mango. Set aside.

2. In a small saucepan, combine the sugar, vinegar, garlic, ginger, and cayenne. Warm over medium-low heat, and allow to simmer for about 10 to 15 minutes until the sugar is dissolved and the mixture thickens slightly.

3. Add the grated mango. Simmer for about 15 minutes until the mango has broken down and the chutney has a jelly-like consistency.

Gluten free **D**airy free

Vegetarian **V**egan

Makes 150 grams of chutney
Time: 40 minutes

Desserts and drinks

Fruit is often served as dessert at the end of a meal. But India is also known for its sweet and creamy puddings and custards. Drinks, enjoyed any time of day, are often sweet as well. The traditional Indian spices make their way into drinks and desserts, adding interesting aromas and flavours.

Mango fool

The British brought many traditions to India. This dessert is one of them. Fools are combinations of pureed fruit and cream. In India, mangoes make this a bright, refreshing dessert.

Ingredients

2 ripe mangoes cut into chunks

1 teaspoon lemon juice

4 teaspoons sugar (optional)

1 cup heavy whipping cream

Tools

Measuring jug and spoons

Blender or food processor

Bowls

Electric hand mixer

Steps

1. Puree the mango and lemon juice in a blender or food processor until smooth. If the mango isn't sweet enough, add sugar a teaspoon at a time to adjust the sweetness. Set aside.

2. Whip the cream with a hand mixer until the cream forms stiff peaks.

3. Stir the pureed mango and cream together.

4. Spoon into glasses and serve.

Quick tip

Whipped cream has reached the stiff peak stage when you can turn the bowl upside down without the mixture falling out.

Makes 4 servings
Time: 10 minutes

Variation

Try this recipe with any frozen or fresh fruit you like.

 luten free

 egetarian

Rice pudding

This creamy pudding is called *kheer* in India. It is a treat often served at special ceremonies and festive occasions. But you can make any meal special by ending with this traditional dessert.

Ingredients	Tools
1.2 litres whole milk	Kitchen scales
65 g basmati rice, cleaned and rinsed	Measuring jug and spoons
	Saucepan
100 g sugar	Mixing spoon
½ teaspoon ground cardamom	Bowl
25 g flaked almonds	Cling film
50 g raisins	

Steps

1. In a large saucepan, bring the milk to the boil, uncovered, on medium heat. It will take about 10 minutes.

2. Add the rice. Bring it back to the boil, then reduce the heat and let simmer for about 1 hour. Stir it often. The rice will turn soft as it absorbs all the milk.

3. Take the rice off the heat. Stir in the sugar and cardamom.

4. Place the mixture in a bowl and set aside to cool to room temperature. Then cover the bowl with cling film, and put in the refrigerator for about 1 hour.

5. Just before serving, stir in the almonds and raisins.

Quick tip

Watch while you wait. Milk can boil over easily, so make sure you don't turn the heat up too high. Rice can stick to the bottom of the pan while it cooks. So stir it frequently.

Makes 4 servings
Time: 2 hours 15 minutes

 Vegetarian Gluten free Nuts contains

Sweet lassi

Lassis are cold, refreshing drinks made with yogurt. They are enjoyed by many Indians, especially in the north. Lassi can be salty, sweet, or fruity. It cools you off whether you are eating a spicy meal, or need a break from a hot, sunny day.

Ingredients	Tools
240 ml plain fat free yogurt	Measuring jug and spoons
60 ml milk	
1½ tablespoons sugar	Blender
About 5 ice cubes (plus more for serving)	Glasses

Steps

1. In a blender, combine the yogurt, sugar, milk, and ice cubes. Blend until smooth.

2. Fill two glasses with ice cubes. Pour the lassi over the cubes.

Makes 2 servings
Time: 5 minutes

Gluten free   Vegetarian

Chai

Chai (tea) is considered the national drink in India. India is the world's second-largest producer of tea. Indians drink tea throughout the entire day. This sweet tea is made with milk and brewed with spices.

Ingredients

240 ml water
2 black tea bags
240 ml milk
Sugar to taste

Spices

1 small cinnamon stick
4 whole cloves
5 cardamom pods, crushed

Tools

Measuring jug
Saucepan
Sieve
Mugs

Steps

1. Place the water, tea bags, and spices in a saucepan. Bring to the boil over high heat.

2. Turn the heat to medium. Add the milk and bring to the boil.

3. Turn off the heat, cover, and let the tea steep for 5 minutes.

4. Pour the tea through a sieve into a measuring jug.

5. Pour the tea into two mugs. Add sugar to taste.

VARIATION

If you don't have whole spices, you can use ground ones for this recipe instead. Replace the spices listed above with ½ teaspoon ground cinnamon, ½ teaspoon ground cardamom, and ¼ teaspoon ground cloves. You'll have flecks of spice in your drink even after you drain it – and lots of flavour!

Makes 2 servings
Time: 10 minutes

 Gluten free Vegetarian

Glossary

Tools

cheesecloth	light, cotton cloth used to strain liquids from foods
chopping board	flat work surface that protects worktops from knife marks when cutting food
colander	bowl-shaped tool with holes for draining liquid from foods
frying pan	pan with a long handle and low sides for use on the hob
grater	flat metal tool with small blades used to cut foods into small strips
grill	device on a cooker that cooks food from above
kitchen scales	device used to measure the weight of food ingredients
measuring jug and spoons	A measuring jug is marked with lines along the side to measure liquids. Measuring spoons come in different sizes to help you measure accurate amounts.
saucepan	pan with a long handle, lid, and high sides for use on the hob
sieve	utensil with a bowl-shaped wire or plastic mesh held in a frame, used for straining liquid from foods
spatula	utensil with a flat end used to flip food over or remove it from a pan
stockpot	large, round metal pot with handles on each side and a lid for use on the hob
whisk	tool used to break down ingredients and bring air into a mixture

Terms

boil	heat a liquid until bubbles rise to the surface
condiment	food that adds additional flavour served alongside a dish
devein	remove the vein from the back of a prawn with a knife
garnish	add food as a decoration to a dish
grill	cook under a grill
knead	mix dough by folding it in half and flattening it with the heel of your hand
mince	cut into very fine pieces
puree	grind or mash ingredients until smooth
sauté	cook in a pan with a little fat, such as oil or butter
savoury	not sweet
simmer	cook over low heat so that the liquid bubbles gently, but does not boil
staple	basic or common ingredient
steep	soak herbs or spices in a liquid to give the liquid flavour
tenderize	break down and soften meat fibres
thaw	warm up to soften
to taste	amount that tastes best to you
whisk	beat quickly with a whisk to break down ingredients and bring air into a mixture

Find out more

Books

India (Been There!), Annabel Savery (Franklin Watts, 2011)

India (Countries Around the World), Ali Brownlie Bojang (Raintree, 2011)

India (Countries in Our World), Darryl Humble (Franklin Watts, 2013)

India (Food and Celebrations), Sylvia Goulding (Wayland, 2012)

India (Looking at Countries), Jillian Powell (Franklin Watts, 2010)

DVDs

Rick Stein's India (BBC), Rick Stein (2entertain, 2013)

The Story of India with Michael Wood (BBC DVD), Michael Wood (2entertain, 2007)

Websites

Food Standards Agency
www.food.gov.uk / multimedia / pdfs / kitchen-check-yppack.pdf
Play these fun puzzles to help you stay safe in the kitchen.

The eatwell plate
food.gov.uk / scotland / scotnut / eatwellplate / #.UevoDNKsiSo
This site describes a healthy, balanced way to get all the nutrients you need in the right proportions.

National Geographic Kids: India
kids.nationalgeographic.com / kids / places / find / india
View videos, look at maps, and read lots of information on this interactive site.

Time for Kids: India
www.timeforkids.com / destination / india
Visit this site to see lots of pictures, learn some Hindi, and follow an Indian girl through her day.

Further research

If this book gave you a taste for Indian food, there are many more Indian cookbooks you could look at. You could also locate Indian restaurants in your own town or city to try a bite of authentic Indian dishes.

You may also be curious about India's history and culture. Visit your local library and ask a librarian to help you learn more. Or ask a parent to help you look up websites for recipes, museums, or other information about India.

Index

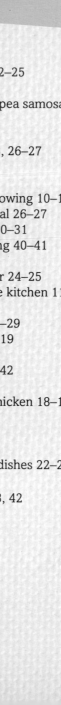